This book belongs to:

Color With Me!

Mom & Me

The Christmas Shop Coloring Book

Sandy Mahony
Mary Lou Brown

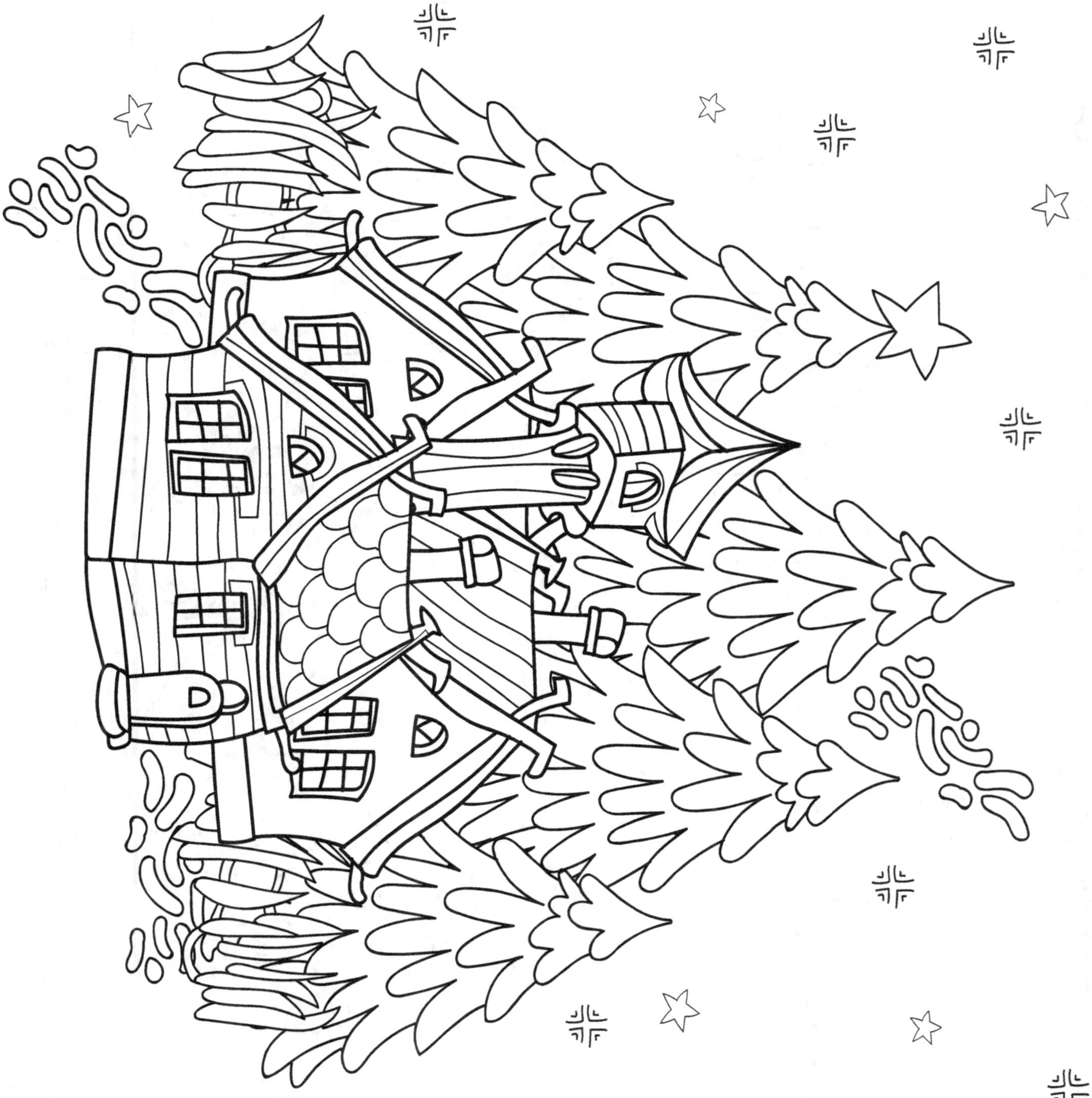

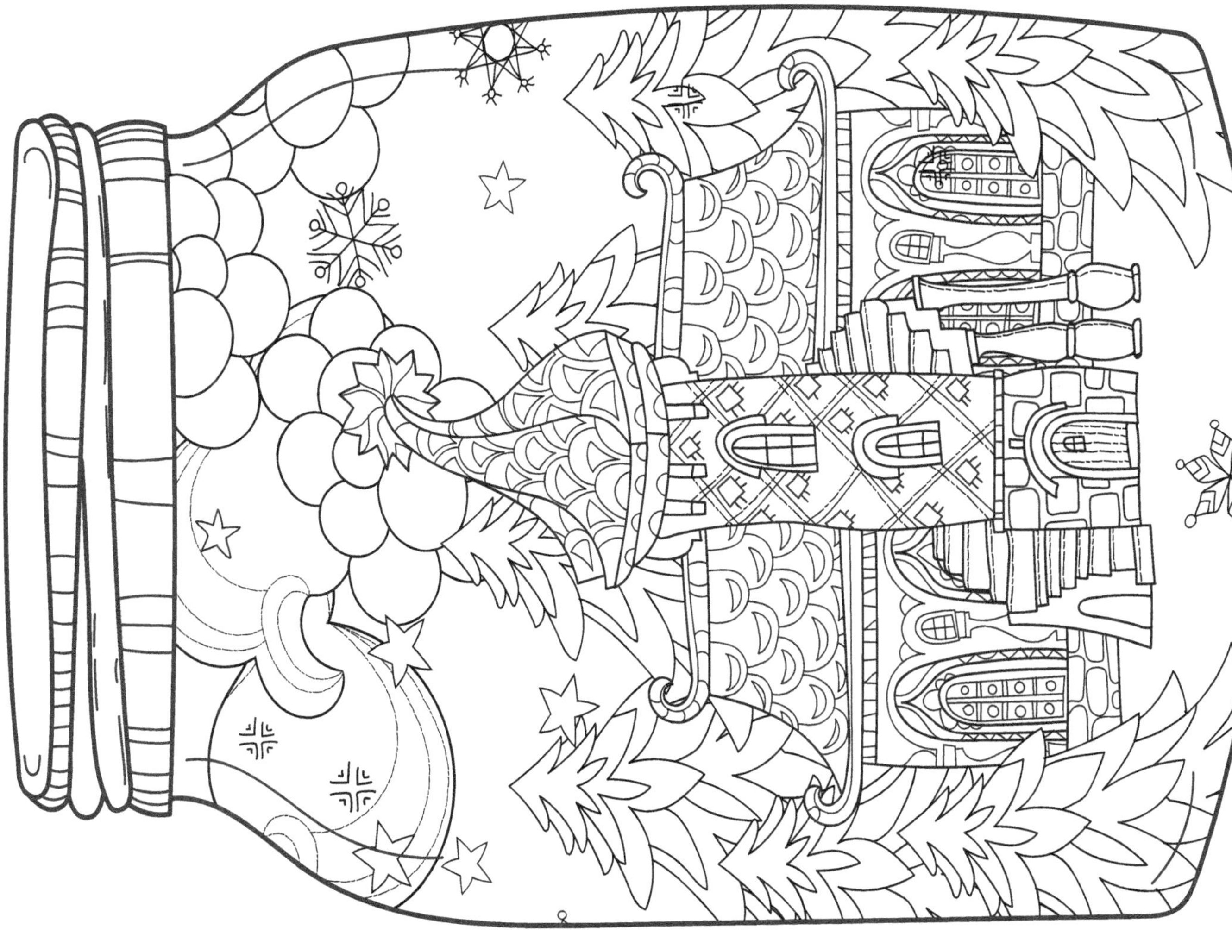

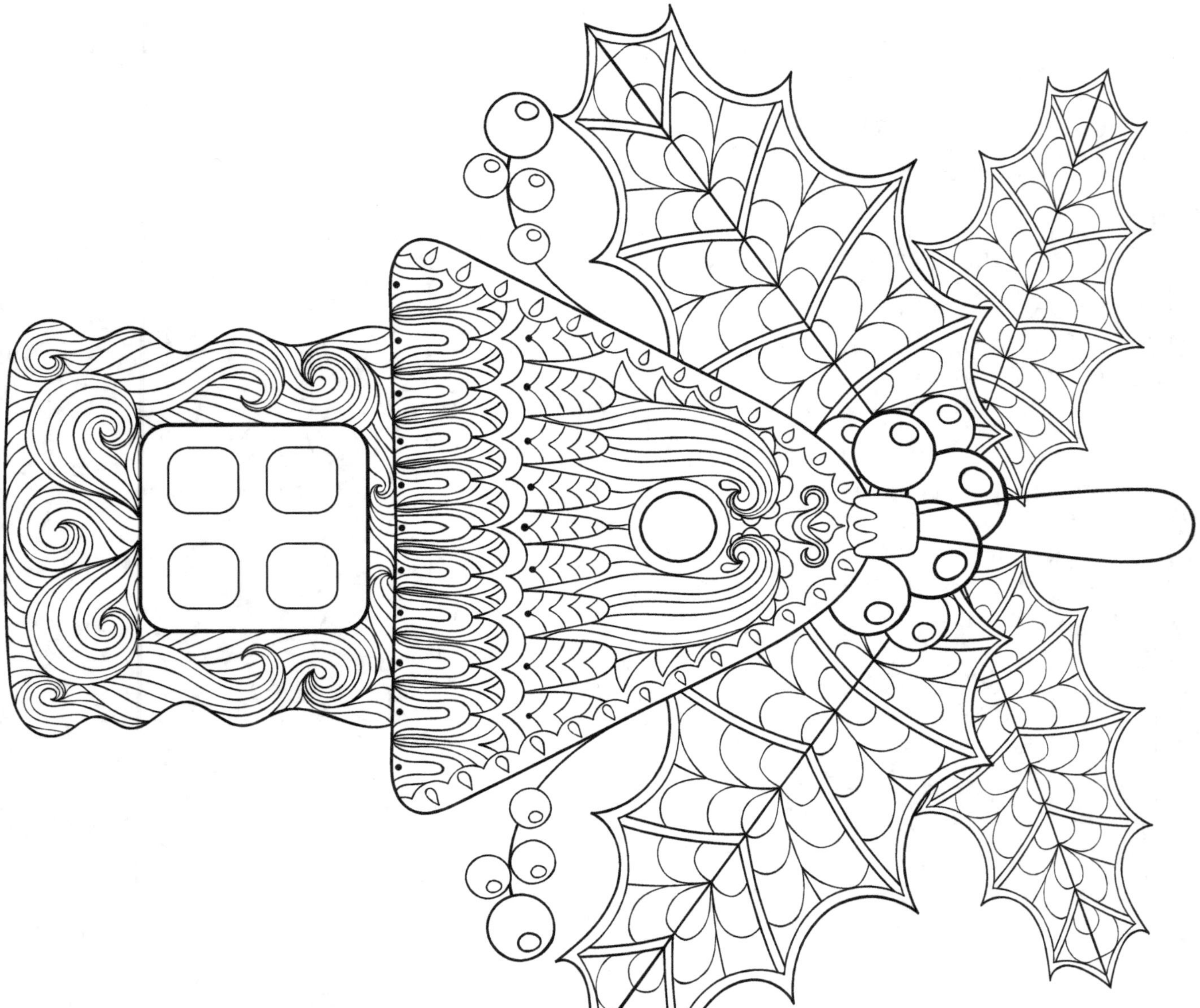

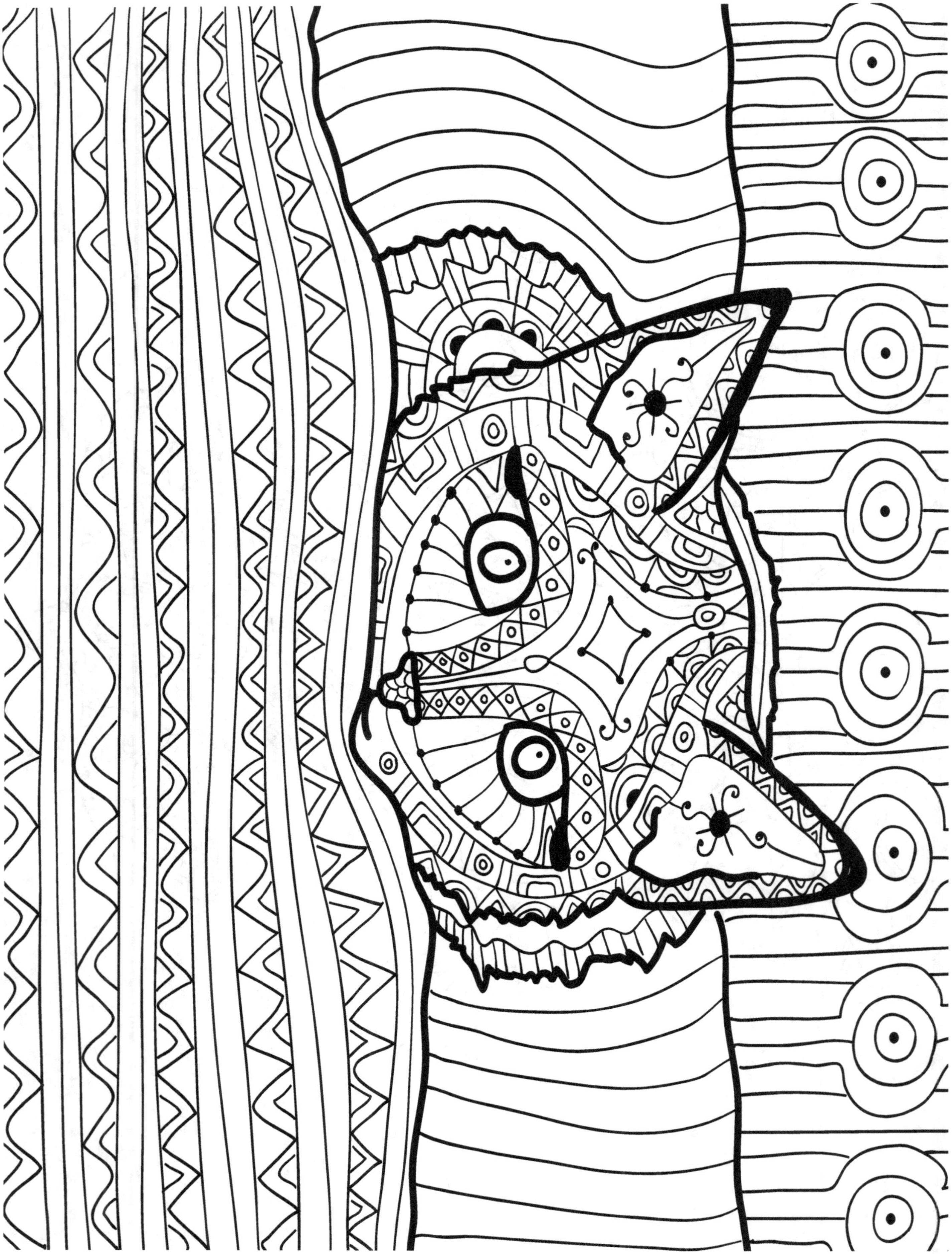

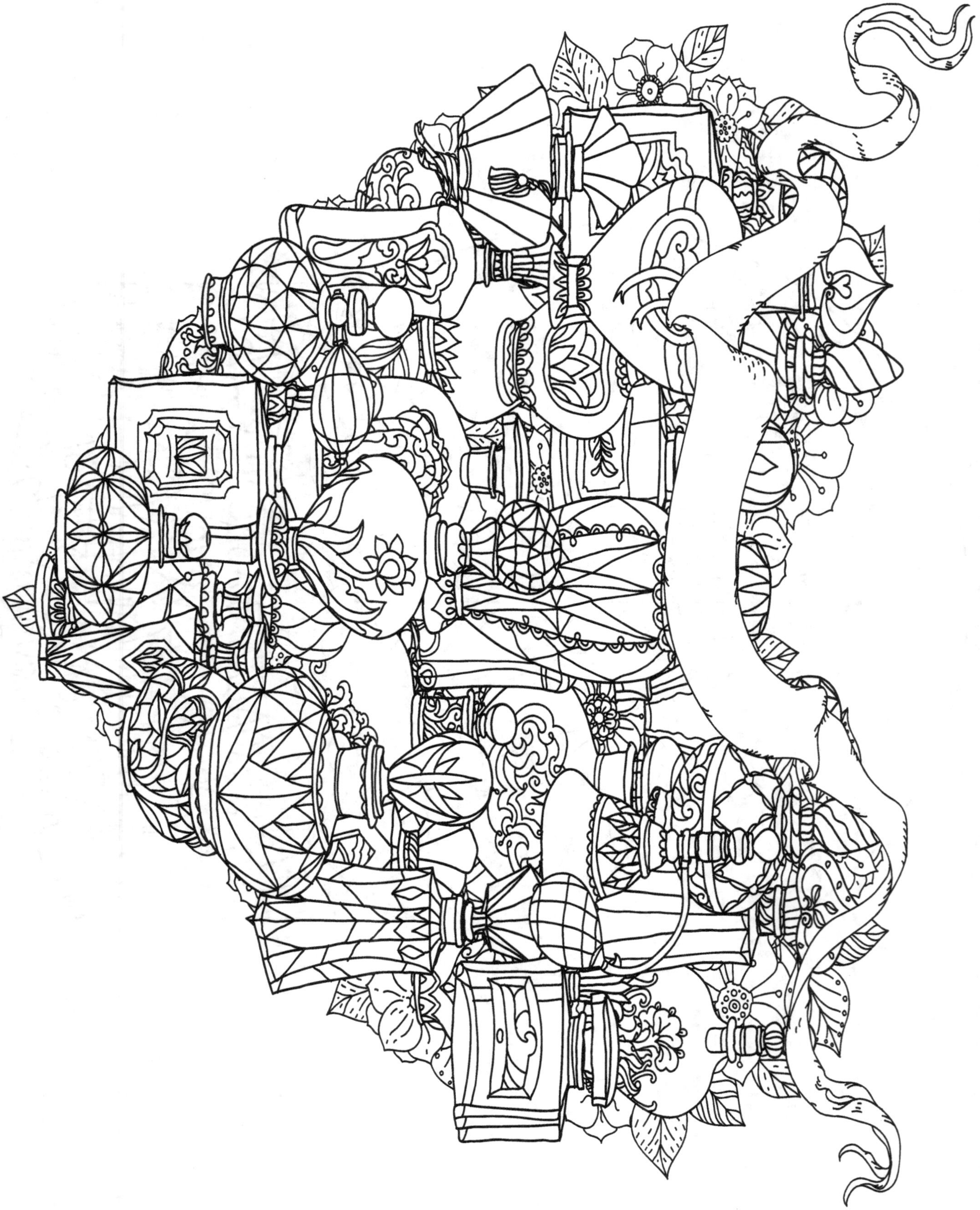

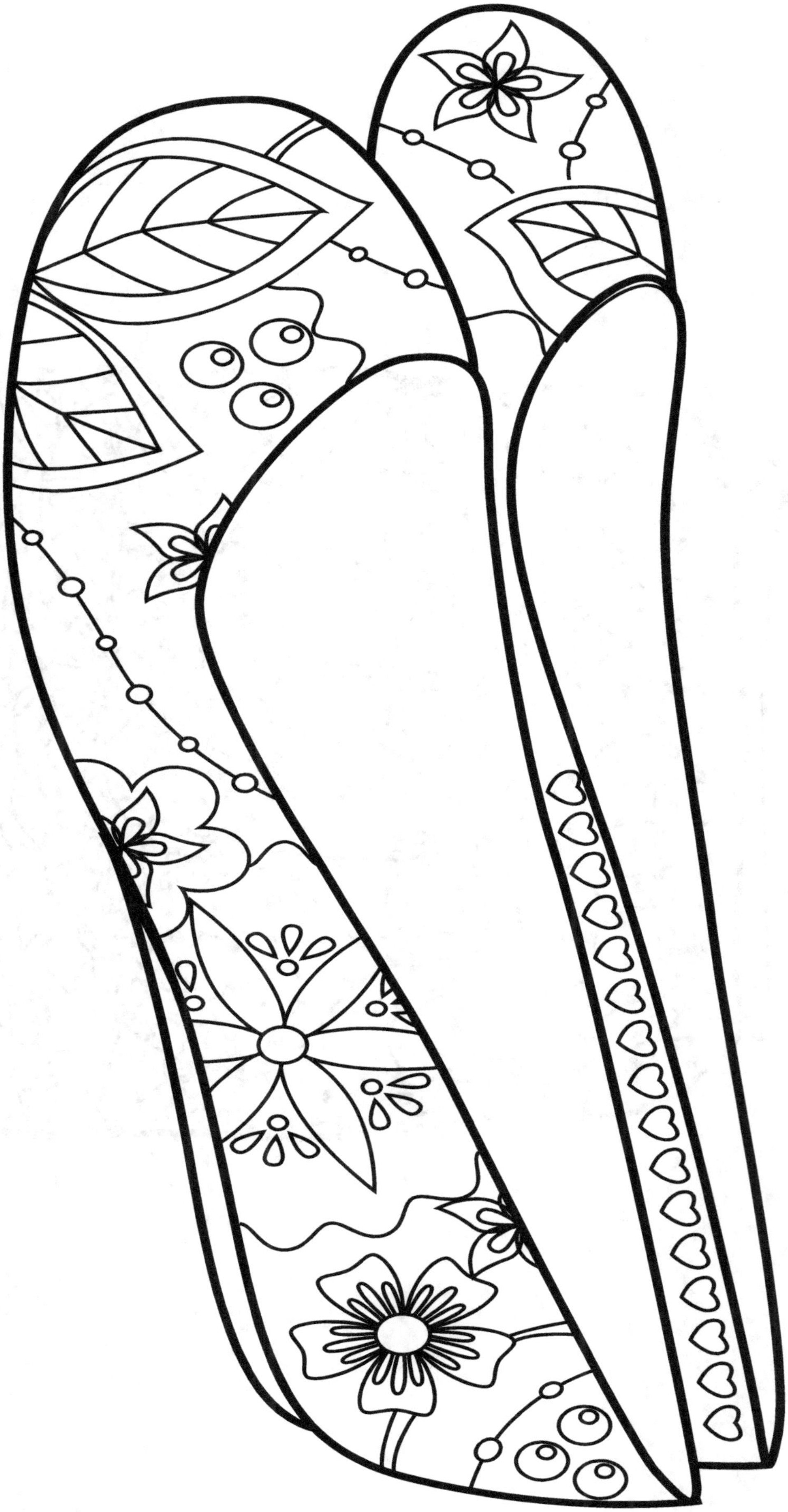

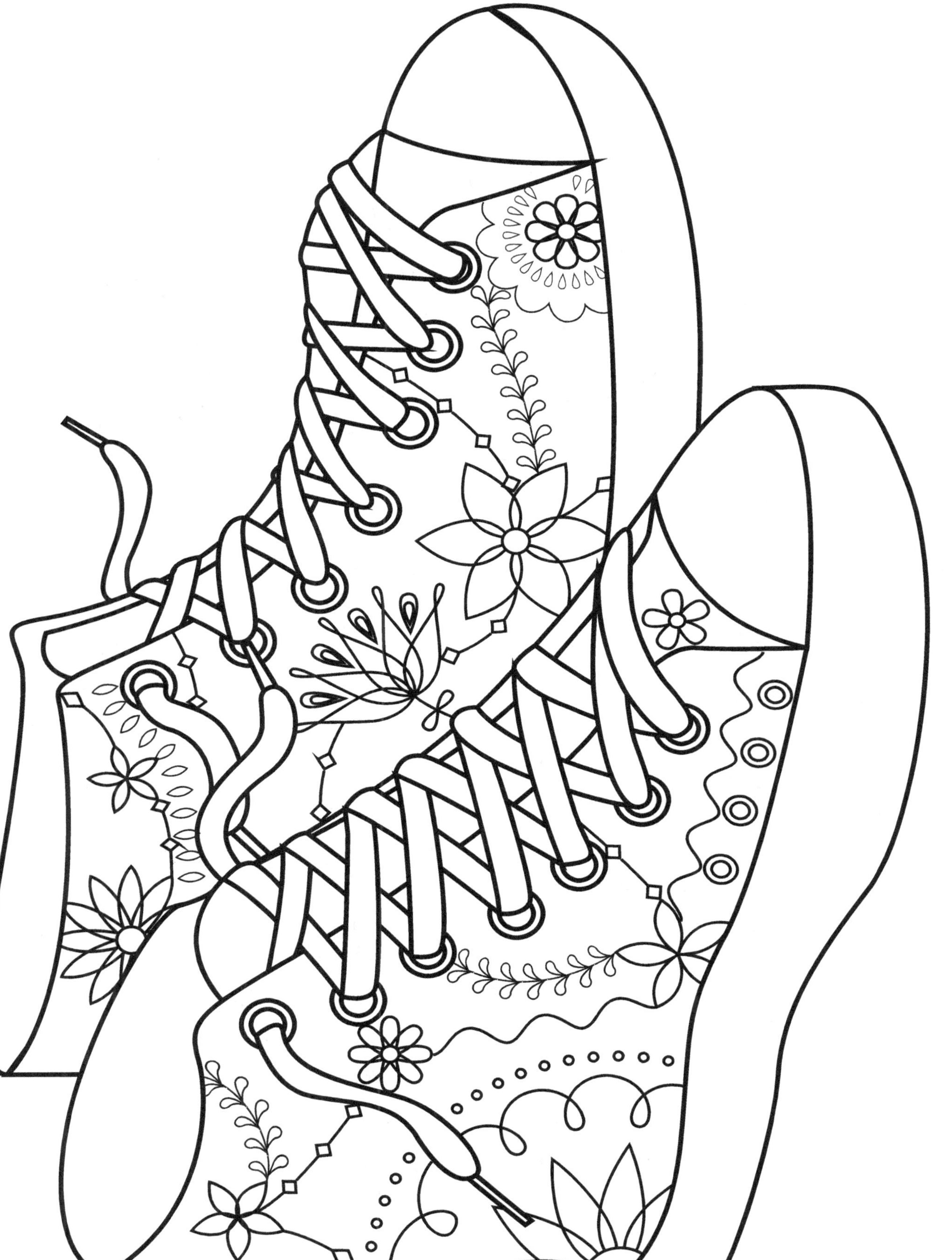

Merry
Christmas
Happy
New
Year!

Merry Christmas!

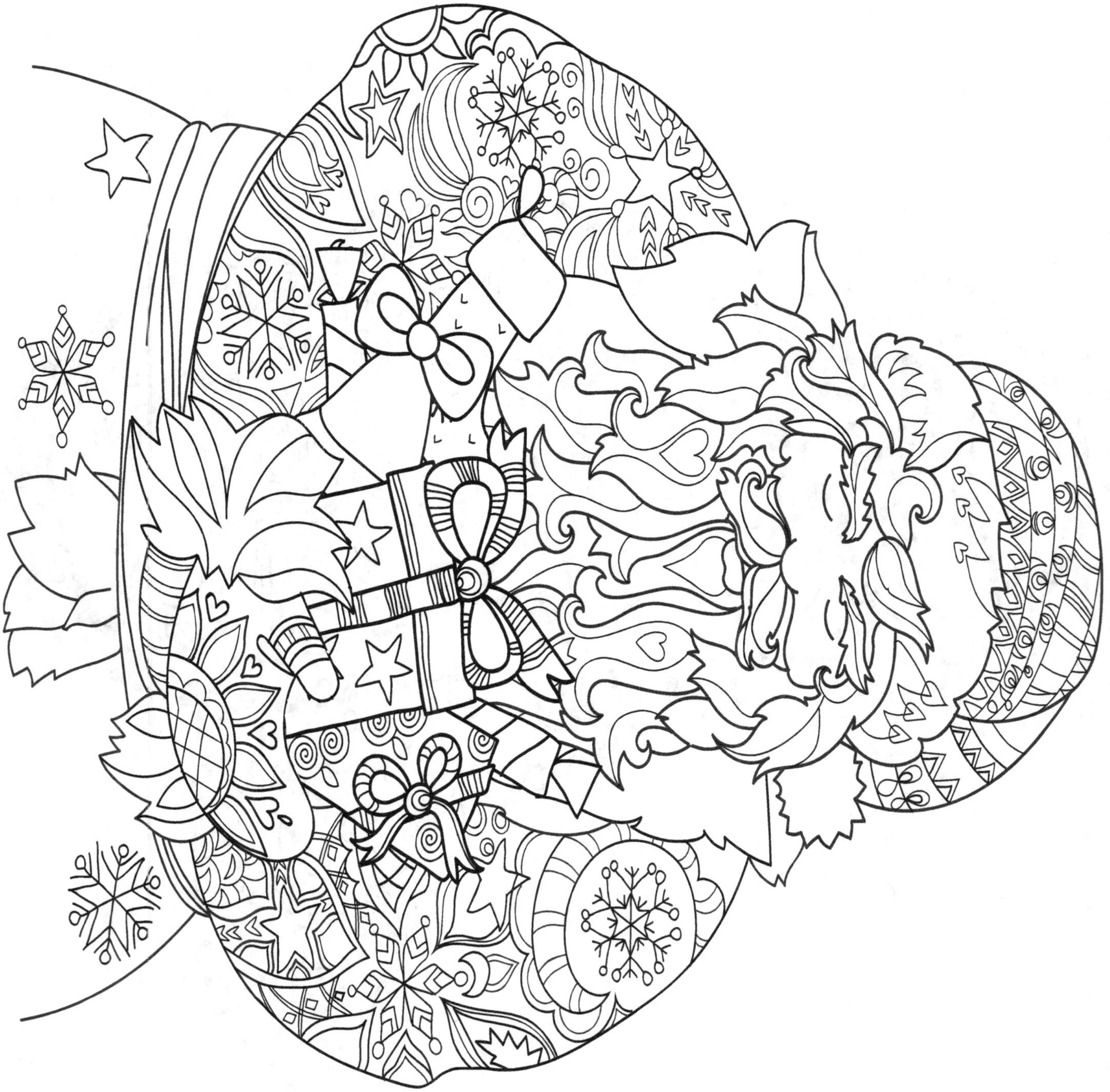

Merry
Christmas

Christmas

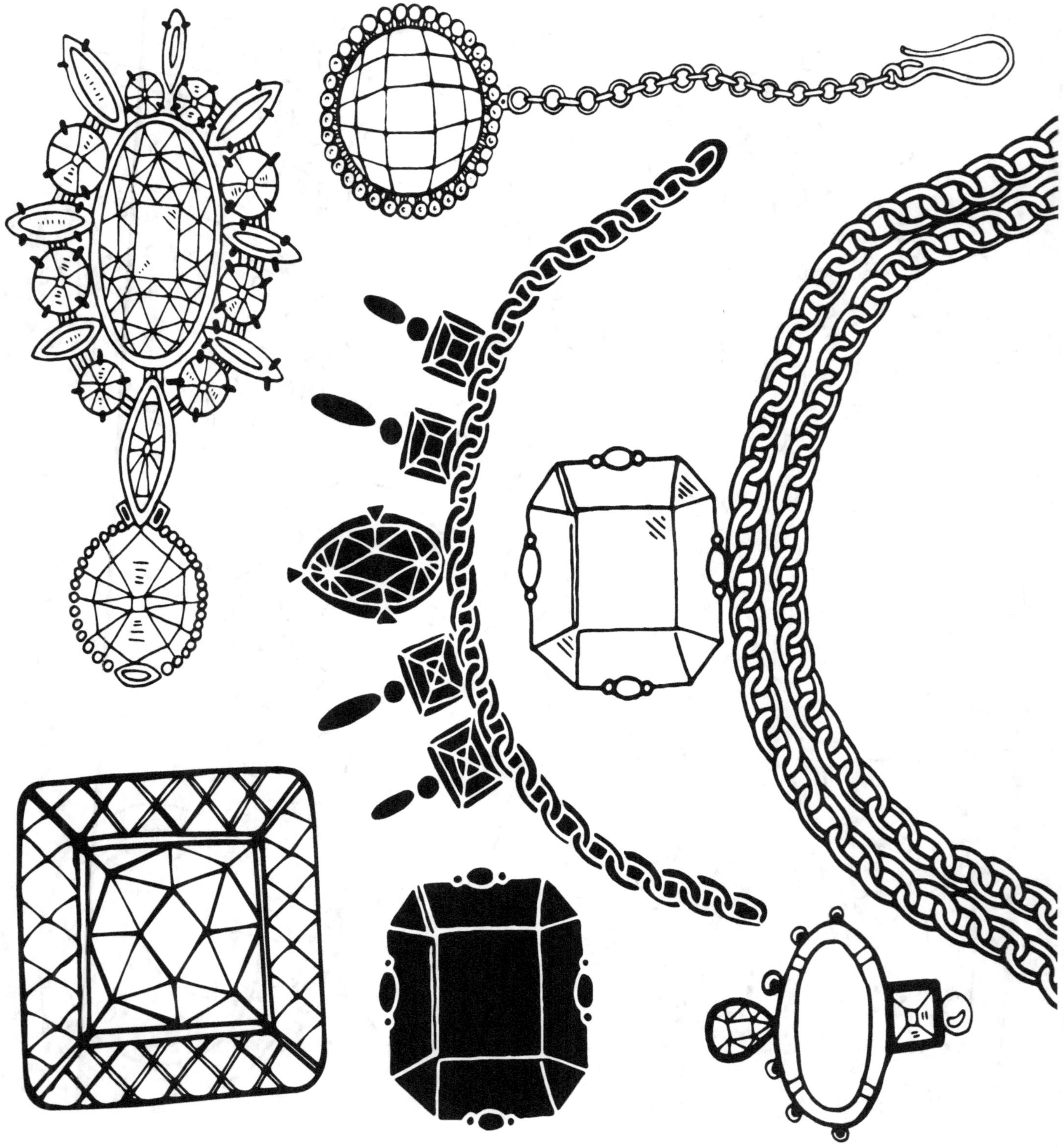

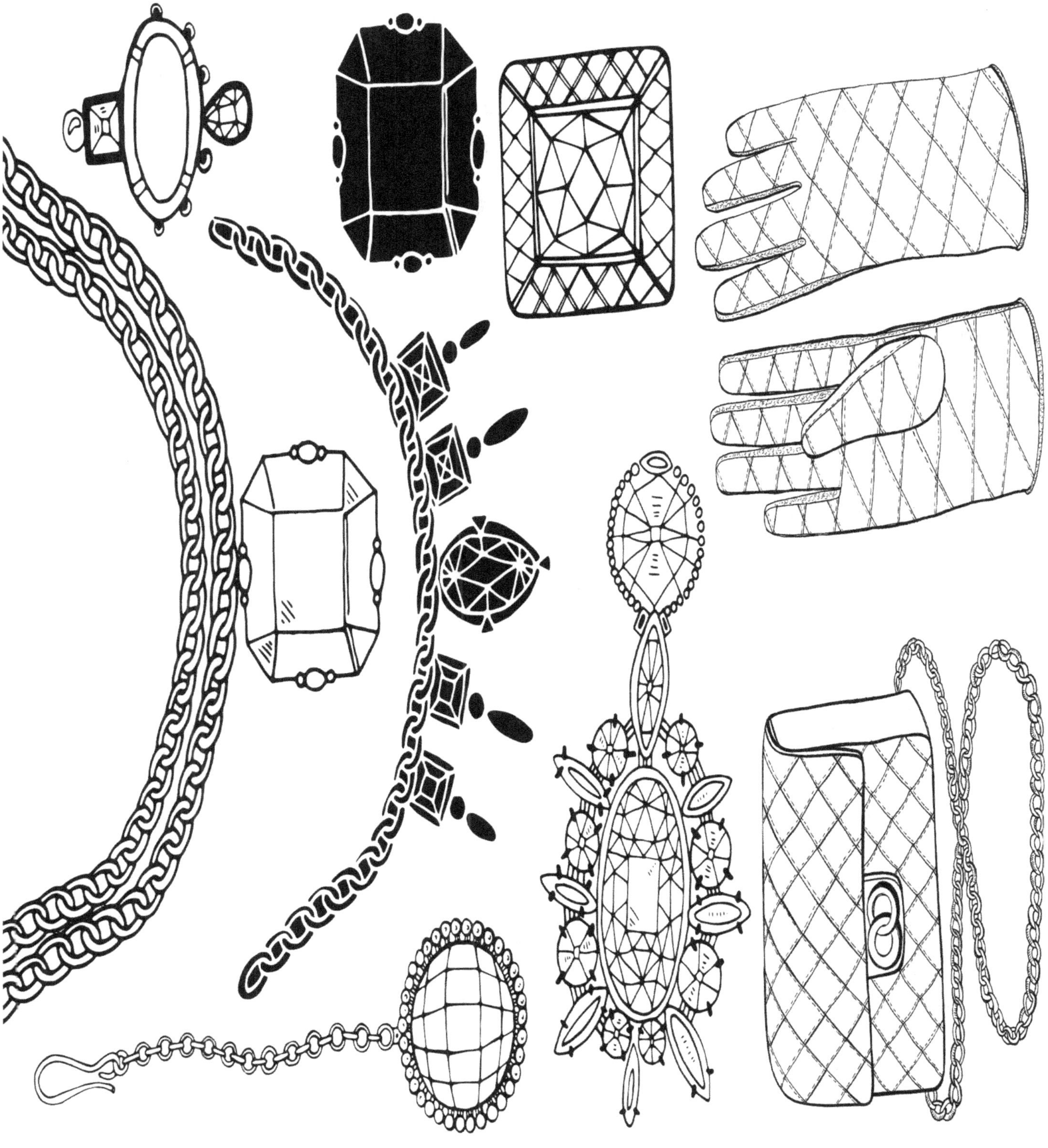

www.ingramcontent.com/pod-product-compliance
Lightning Source LLC
Chambersburg PA
CBHW081800280526
45789CB00008B/2937
9781540534002